Manage Like Abraham Lincoln

Table of Contents

Introduction

Abraham Lincoln is known for his story telling.

According to his friends, Lincoln usually began all of his stories by saying, "That reminds me of a story…" And, once he started talking everyone would move in real close, so they could hear what "Old Abe" had to say.

While Lincoln's stories, more often than not, made people laugh, they almost always had a point to them.

The stories were Lincoln's way of making it easy for people to understand what he was saying. Yes. He could have just said what he wanted to say, but Lincoln knew that most people quickly forget what they're told.

Stories have a way of sticking with you, and driving the point home.

Over the past year, I've taken the time to read hundreds of Lincoln's stories, sayings, and quotes from his letters, and what really stands out to me, is his deep understanding of people. Many of his stories ring just as true today, as they did when he first told them over 150 years ago.

For business leaders, they also possess some valuable information on how to manage your business, your employees, and your personal relationships with friends and family.

What I've done for this book is to pick out twenty-five of my favorite Lincoln stories and sayings, and present them along with examples of how they can help you solve your everyday business problems.

My suggestion is to read through them all. Then read one a day, until you can master the knowledge they teach.

At the end of the book, after the stories, you will find a short review of the situation Lincoln found himself in when he became President, and about how he managed his soldiers, and his generals.

With all of the violence and destruction going on around him, Lincoln never once lost his temper with any of his charges. Instead he took time to learn how he could help them, and used his stories to help share his wisdom.

Stand up for what you believe

One day a group of politicians visited President Lincoln telling him what a disgrace General Grant was. They said he was vulgar, and a drunk, and should be removed from command of the army.

Finally, the politicians, seeing that Lincoln remained unconvinced, said they "would get him proof."

"You needn't waste your time getting proof," quipped Lincoln, "you just find out to oblige me, what brand of whisky Grant drinks, because I want to send a barrel of it to each of my generals."

This is one of my favorite Lincoln stories. Ministers, Congressman, Senators, and just about all of Lincoln's political advisors wanted him to get rid of Grant. Everyone complained he was a drunkard, he was loud, belligerent, uncouth, and his language was vulgar.

Lincoln would listen thoughtfully to all of these complaints, but none of them ever swayed his faith in Grant, because Grant wasn't afraid to fight.

He went into battle often, and more importantly he won.

Take a minute to think about your best employees. Many of them probably have habits you or someone else in the company isn't fond of. Someone may have even suggested you fire or demote old so-and-so, because of this or that.

Some bosses will agree with the complainer that those are bad habits, or the person should be fired. Some bosses might even go so far as to fire the person, because that is what the majority wants.

Lincoln could surely have done that with Grant as the complaints piled up against him, but Lincoln saw through the general's rough exterior. He recognized Grant was just the man he needed for the job. He was a fighter, and when he saw an opportunity to advance, he took it. He didn't second guess himself, and sit on the side lines because he wasn't sure what would happen.

Lincoln believed in Grant, and understood he was the right man for the job, no matter what everyone else thought.

The next time someone comes to you complaining about one of your employees, because he does this or that, have the courage to stand up for him, even if you're the only one who will.

Pay attention to details

Back in the early days of his career as a frontier lawyer, Lincoln was engaged in an important trial.

It was a really hot day. His opponent was arguing his case, and as he paced around he was starting to sweat, so the man removed his jacket and vest. The lawyer's shirt buttoned in the back, not in the front, as was customary.

Lincoln was quick to notice the discrepancy, and said to the jury –

"Gentlemen of the jury, having justice on my side, I don't think you will at all be influenced by the gentleman's pretended knowledge of law, when you see he does not even know which side of his shirt should be in front."

Lincoln's story drew a laugh from the jury and the audience, and won him the case.

Moral of the story: Pay attention to the details. Sometimes the smallest things will bring you the biggest rewards.

A lot of leaders will tell you they look at the big picture. As long as everything is running well, they're not going to sweat the small details.

But, as the old saying goes often times "the devil's in the details."

Back in the early days of the personal computer, IBM was the industry leader. In the early eighties they had just released the personal computer, and it was taking the business world by storm. They were so sure the profit was all in the hardware, and software was just a minor accessory.

In their carelessness, they sold the software that ran their computers to an unknown Harvard dropout named Bill Gates, and they learned the hard way the computer business is driven by applications, not by the hardware.

The fact is: They were so convinced their business was all about computers they overlooked it was software that ran those very computers.

The next time you're brainstorming business ideas, keep in mind – "the devil is in the details."

Often times, the smallest things, lead to the biggest rewards.

Don't be afraid to laugh at yourself

One story tells about a man sticking a gun in Lincoln's face.

"What seems to be the matter," inquired Lincoln.

"Well," replied the stranger, "some years ago I swore that if I ever came across an uglier man than myself, I'd shoot him on the spot."

A much relieved Lincoln is said to have replied, "Shoot me, for if I am an uglier man than you, I don't want to live."

I've also heard the story where the man has a knife, or a really big stick.

The take away is the same: There are always going to be people who want to make fun of you for one thing, or another. It's a lot easier to laugh with them, than argue against them.

Lincoln was used to hearing stories about his looks. He stood six foot, four inches tall, weighed only 180 pounds, had ears that were too big for his head, legs that were too long for his body, and skin like leather. Common comments on his appearance, described him as gaunt and homely.

He'd learned long ago it was a lot easier to join in the fun than argue the point.

So many people get mad when someone says something about them. Those of us who were bullied in elementary school know the secret to handling this: If you laugh with them, they eventually look for another target.

At the start of my business career, I managed a convenience store. People would get screaming mad when I refused to sell them beer or cigarettes. I mean these people would just blow their tops, screaming at the top of their lungs to f—k off, and die. They'd tear you and your mom, and uncle and aunt, and anybody else they could think of apart. And, every time, I'd just look them in the eye, give them a big old smile, and say, "Thank-you, have a nice day!"

It would just freak them out, because there was nothing else they could say.

People make fun of you for one reason: They want to get your temper flaring. If you can show them it doesn't bother you, the games over.

Keep it simple stupid

One day Lincoln gave his law partner some advice on how to approach people.

"Billy, don't shoot too high – aim lower, and the common people will understand you.

"They are the ones you want to reach – at least, they are the ones you ought to reach.

"The educated and refined people will understand you anyway. If you aim too high, your idea will only be over the head of the masses, and only reach those who need no hitting."

And, that is the secret of Lincoln's success, he talked to the masses.

Abraham Lincoln knew instinctively the key to communication was to: *Keep It Simple, Stupid.*

A lot of people like to hear the sound of their own voice, and they feel the best way to impress people is to talk a lot, and to use big words.

People still do that today. Many business people feel compelled to use elaborate Power Point presentations to drive home their point. Between the slides, and their high faluting words, most of it flies right over people's heads.

There's a reason newspapers and mass magazines write their stories at the fifth grade level. Everyone can understand it.

Remember this the next time you're giving a talk to the troops, or a sales pitch to that big client, keep it simple. Don't use a five dollar word, when a five cent word will get your point across just as well.

That reminds me of another Lincoln story. Lincoln was in the courtroom arguing a case with another lawyer, when the man asked him, "Isn't that so, Mr. Lincoln?"

Lincoln took a good look at the speaker, and told him, "That depends. If that was a Latin word you used, you better get yourself another jury."

It was Lincoln's way of telling the man, he'd lost his case, because he'd spoken over the heads of his audience.

Of course, there are times you can go out there, and use a lot of those five dollar words, and everyone will understand you, but you better save that talk for an IT convention, or the like. And, the truth is, most of them probably wouldn't mind if you dumbed it down a little, and made things more interesting.

During the war, many politicians and businessmen would visit with the soldiers at the military hospitals.

One gentleman visiting the military hospital in Washington couldn't help overhearing a wounded soldier talking loudly and laughing about President Lincoln. The man followed the trail of laughter to the wounded soldier, and told him, "You must be slightly wounded?"

"Yes," replied the soldier, "very slightly – I have only lost one leg, and I'd be glad enough to lose the other, if I could hear some more of "Old Abe's" stories.

To be a leader, you've got to inspire confidence in your employees.

A lot of leaders stay locked up in their corporate offices reading reports, and letting others tell them what is going on in their business. Lincoln took a different tack, and visited his soldiers – on the battlefields, and in the hospitals.

In the early years of his Presidency, Lincoln was widely lampooned and torn apart by the press, and many of the people around the country. But, his soldiers never doubted him. Lincoln always made time for the common soldiers. He walked among them, shook their hands, told stories to them, and took time to comfort them when they were sick or wounded.

In return, they respected and admired the president.

If you're a leader, and you are not personally visiting and working with all of your employees, from the lowest to the highest level, you're missing the boat.

Abraham Lincoln understood instinctively managing is about people. To effectively manage people, you have to connect with them, one-on-one. Every story I've featured in this book, has Lincoln going out among the people, and visiting with them, asking them questions, and sharing stories with them.

Give the people what they want

There is a story told about a westerner who visited Lincoln at the White House. Like many others who visited Lincoln, he was hoping the President would grant him an office. In this case the man wanted to be the Postmaster in his town.

Noticing that Lincoln looked a little sick, the man inquired about his illness.

"I think it is smallpox," replied the President, "but you needn't worry. I'm only in the first stages."

Upon hearing the word smallpox, the visitor grabbed his hat, and bolted for the door.

Lincoln hollered after him, "What's your hurry."

Later Lincoln told the story to one of his friends, adding –

"Now that's the way people are. When I can't give them what they want, they're dissatisfied, and say harsh things about me, but when I've got something to give to everybody they scamper off."

When you're the boss, people are often going to come to you asking for things you can't possibly give them – promotions, time off, raises, etc. After a while you get tired of telling them no all of the time, and just want to tell them anything you can to make them go away.

Lincoln found a unique way to scare the above gentleman off.

People were always visiting Lincoln at the White House, especially in the early years of his Presidency. They asked him to be appointed to offices, for political favors, for special ranks in the military. There were so many of them asking, and so few positions available.

What Lincoln needed was common soldiers. He could give away as many spots in the army as people wanted, but after the first few years of the war, people grew weary of it, and volunteer ranks shrunk.

Find a way to convince people to fill the positions you have open, and to buy the products you have available. In the long run it's a win-win situation for both of you.

Take a minute to think about it

An old friend from Springfield visited Lincoln at the White House shortly after he became President seeking to be made Superintendent of the Mint.

Lincoln had no choice but to turn the man down. He had no qualifications for the position.

Afterwards Lincoln said –

"Well, now, I never thought Mr. ___ had anything more than average ability when we were young men together. But, then, I suppose he thought the same thing about me, and here I am!"

Lincoln recognized the obvious. Life is funny sometimes, and growing up, we never know where we will end up.

Moral of the story: Treat everybody with respect. The guy you fire today might be the guy who is hiring you at your next job. The poorly dressed kid everybody else is making fun of in math class, might just be the next Bill Gates.

Lincoln was clever enough to know things aren't always what you think they are. We all have perceptions about the people around us, but a lot of that is based upon first impressions. Lincoln didn't think his old friend had the ability needed for the job, but he could understand the same thing could be said about him.

Think about it next time you meet with somebody. You might not think they're going anywhere today, but next week, or next year, you never know who they might become.

Show respect to everyone you come in contact with. Treat them with respect. It's not just good manners. That annoying guy, or gal, sitting in the cubicle next to you just might be the next President, of your company, or of the United States.

Stranger things have happened!

Don't give up to soon

General Meade was widely acclaimed as the hero of Gettysburg, and after that success one of the general's friends told Lincoln that he should be made Commander-in-Chief of the Union Army.

"Now don't misunderstand me," Lincoln told the man. "I am profoundly grateful down to the bottom of my boots for what he did at Gettysburg, but I think that if I had been General Meade, I would have fought another battle."

Lincoln understood what many people didn't. Although Meade had made a major victory for the Union, he could have ended the war, if he hadn't stopped to rest on his laurels.

Salesman hit this same barrier every day. They make a big sale early in the day, or they reach their quota, and they go home for the day thinking they did a great job. But, the best salesmen look at that big score as motivation to move forward, and hit another homerun.

If I could say anything on this point, it would be this: Celebrate your victories, but before you do, know what you could be celebrating.

Too often in life, we stop just short of reaching our full potential.

Don't let worries hold you back

Slavery was a big issue in Lincoln's life, and a clergyman back in Springfield once asked him, "What was to be his policy on the slave issue..."

Lincoln replied, "You know Father B., the old Methodist preacher? And you know Fox River and its freshets?

Well, once in the presence of Father B., a young Methodist was worrying about Fox River, and expressing fears that he should be prevented from fulfilling some of his appointments by a freshet in the river."

Father B. checked him in his gravest manner. Said he: "Young man, I have always made it a rule in my life, not to cross Fox River till I get to it."

"And," said Mr. Lincoln, "I am not going to worry myself over the slavery question till I get to it."

Too often, we are paralyzed by fear of the unknown. We're so busy worrying about what might happen we don't do the things we should do.

Let me give you an example: Weather seems to be my Achilles heel. Whenever it's getting ready to storm outside, I start thinking the worst, that I'm going to get caught in it. As a result, I cancel my plans. My daughter often makes fun of me, letting me know she's not afraid of a little weather.

Business people have the same problem. We create imaginary barriers. Quotas, or sales goals, can often become a scary number. Say your goal this quarter is to increase sales by 10 percent, and your branch has never done better than 3 percent. A lot of people are going to be fixated by that number and put all sorts of imaginary barriers in their path.

Opening a new branch in an area where you've never had good sales or where you were forced out of the market several decades before, can create the same imaginary barriers.

Lincoln knew the best way to deal with imaginary barriers: Don't worry about them. Instead, tell yourself you will cross that barrier, if and when, you come to it.

Lincoln on Ambition

"Every man is said to have his peculiar ambition. Whether it be true or not, I can say, for one, that I have no other so great as that of being truly esteemed of my fellow-men, by rendering myself worthy of their esteem."

Some men desire money, some power, Lincoln's ambition was to be worthy of esteem by his fellow men.

What's your ambition?

Money and power will only get you so far, they can disappear as quickly as they come, and in the end no one will remember you for how much money or power you have. They will remember you for the person you were.

How do you want to be remembered?

Compliment people – often

"Everyone likes a compliment. Thank you for yours."

Think about that for a minute. "Everyone likes a compliment."

When someone tells you, "you look great" or "great job," it changes your whole day.

If you learn only one thing from this entire book, learn to compliment people, and do if often. If you must, go out of your way, and search hard for a way to compliment everyone you come across. It will brighten their day, and in the long run, it will enrich your day as well.

Turn it around

At one of the Lincoln Douglas debates, Stephen Douglas told the crowd that when he first met Mr. Lincoln he was a grocery-keeper, and sold whisky, cigars, etc. "Mr. L.," he said, "was a very good bartender."

Lincoln's quick reply was, "What Mr. Douglas has said gentlemen, is true enough; I did keep a grocery, and I did sell cotton, candles, and cigars, and sometimes whisky; but I remember in those days that Mr. Douglas was one of my best customers. Many a time have I stood on one side of the counter and sold whisky to Mr. Douglas on the other side; but the difference between us now is: I have left my side of the counter, but Mr. Douglas still sticks to his as tenaciously as ever."

In less than one hundred words, Lincoln turned the whole argument against him around, and gave the crowd good reason to laugh at his opponent.

The next time someone says or does something about you, think of a way you can politely turn the tables around on them.

Let's say you're up for a promotion. Your rival for the job, Johnson, just reminded the board about that time two years ago when he beat you in the sales contest, and brought in five more accounts than you did.

Pause for a moment, and think about the situation. Johnson did beat you. You can't deny that, but what if four of his bigger accounts quickly defected to another agency, because he couldn't service them properly; or perhaps, you brought in fewer accounts than Johnson, but your customers made the company a twenty percent higher profit.

Do what Lincoln did, acknowledge what your opponent said was true, then turn the tables around, and show how your accomplishment was more valuable to the company.

You never know who you're talking to

At the height of the Civil War you could often times find Abraham Lincoln walking the streets of Washington all by himself, without bodyguards or attendants.

On one such day, Lincoln met a crippled soldier while walking between the White House and the War Department. This soldier was obviously down on his luck, and Lincoln could hear the man cursing the President, the Government, the war, and his life.

Lincoln approached the man, and asked him, "What's the matter."

The soldier told him that he was very discouraged, and was having trouble getting his pay. Lincoln told him he knew something about the law, and would try to help him out.

Lincoln examined the soldier's papers, and wrote a note on the back, telling him to take it to Mr. Potts, the chief clerk at the War Department. After that Lincoln left.

The soldier's friends meanwhile had ducked behind some nearby bushes when they saw the President talking with their friend. When Lincoln left they asked the man if he knew who that was he was talking to?

The soldier replied, rather matter of factly, "Some ugly old man who pretended to be a lawyer!"

His friends had him turn his papers over to look at what the man had written, "Mr. Potts, attend to this man's case at once, and see that he gets his pay. A. L."

Sometimes you really don't know who you're talking to.

I'm reminded of the overaggressive driver who was racing off to his job interview. He was running a few minutes late, and he started zigzagging through cars as he got closer to his goal. When he reached the building he was going to, he jumped into a parking spot another car was starting to pull into. On the way into the office, the lady from that car was close behind him, and in his rush he let the door slam in her face.

At the reception desk, he swaggered up to the secretary and told her he had a 9:15 appointment with Miss Henson, as he watched the twice slighted lady walk down the hallway.

Five minutes later, Miss Henson came out to get him, and you guessed it, she was the lady from the parking lot.

It's easy to take advantage of someone, or to not show good manners, but the truth is: You never really know who you're talking to.

Another takeaway from this story: Solve the problems you can.

Lincoln could have told the man who he was, and made a big deal out of the fact he was the President, but he didn't, because that wouldn't have done anything to solve the soldier's problem.

Instead, Lincoln took it upon himself to look over the soldier's papers, and direct him to the man who could take care of his problem.

How often do you hear people complaining about this or that, and just let them walk on by, when a few minutes of time on your part could solve their problem.

Rethink the problem

As a Captain in the Black Hawk War, Abraham Lincoln was having some trouble getting his company through a narrow gate. Scratching his head for a minute, Lincoln finally shouted out to his men –

"This company is dismissed for two minutes, when it will fall in again on the other side."

The simplest solutions really are the best. Sometimes you've got to let your employees work things out for themselves.

A lot of bosses try to micro-manage every situation, and have a standard procedure for every situation that comes up, but by doing that, you sometimes make things a whole lot harder than they need to be.

Your manager in Kalamazoo may have a great way to peel potatoes that works just great for him, and another employee in Des Moines might have the perfect method for selling insurance to dentists.

You'll never know unless you give them the opportunity to try it their way.

Look at the bright side

In the February of 1861, President-elect Lincoln, and Mrs. Lincoln were still in Springfield. After news of Lincoln's election the couple received many congratulatory gifts, especially of clothing.

Lincoln is said to have told his wife,

"Well, wife, if nothing else comes out of this scrape we are going to have some new clothes, are we not?

Everyone is a little nervous before taking on a new position. Lincoln managed to discover the bright side, even if being President wasn't the right fit for him.

Next time you find yourself facing a new job, or responsibility, don't worry about what can go wrong, think about what good will come out of it.

Be careful what you ask for

One time when he was walking around Washington, Lincoln was approached by a tramp who asked him for ten cents so he could get a meal.

"You look like an able bodied man," inquired Lincoln, "why aren't you in the army?"

"They wouldn't take me," said the man. "I'd be glad to die for my country if they gave me the chance."

Hearing that, Lincoln scribbled a note on a piece of paper he was carrying, and told him to take it to the Fifteenth Street recruiting station.

As the man was leaving, Lincoln told him, "If they can't do anything to help you, come back to see me. I'm just walking around."

The man never showed up at the recruiting station, nor did he return to Lincoln.

Here's what the note said:

"Colonel Fielding: The bearer is anxious to go to the front and die for his country. Can't you give him a chance?"

Moral of the story: Be careful what you ask for, you just may get it.

The poor tramp embellished his story, "saying he'd be happy to die for his country," but what the man really wanted was a dime. He didn't want to die for his country that was just some filler he threw in to make it look like he was trying to make a living.

How often do you tell people what you want without making your request perfectly clear?

A lot of times, when we ask people to do something, or give someone else instructions; what we tell them is ambiguous and unclear. We throw in extra details totally unrelated, or contradictory to what we are asking.

Be careful of what you ask for, and make sure you are asking for what you actually want.

Make sure you're on the right side

Early in the war Lincoln was talking with a clergyman:

"Let us have faith, Mr. President," said the minister, "that the Lord is on our side in this great struggle."

Mr. Lincoln quietly answered, "I am not at all concerned about that, for I know that the Lord is always on the side of right; but it is my constant anxiety and prayer that I and this nation may be on the Lord's side."

Make sure you're making the right decision.

Every day in the business world you are forced to make decisions. Often times you're forced to choose between the worst of two evils. Other times you're faced with a moral dilemma that makes you choose between right and wrong.

That reminds me of a story:

Several years ago I worked for a large company. One day I came into work and found out I'd just missed out on watching security drag the branch president, vice president, and controller out of the building.

As the story developed over the next week, we learned the same thing had happened at over half of the local branches around the country, and at the corporate office.

It turns out the company was demanding an unattainable sales goal from its branches, and many of them, rather than show a loss, decided to cook the books, and record false sales to make them look better.

None of these businessman questioned what they were doing was wrong; they just didn't have the courage to put their jobs on the line and turn in bad numbers.

As Lincoln said, make sure you're on the right side of the question.

Do something, do anything

Lincoln often visited his soldiers on the battlefield, and in one such excursion he was making a visit to McClellan's headquarters with a group of Congressman. As they approached the camp, Lincoln told them:

"It is called the Army of the Potomac, but it is only McClellan's bodyguard...If McClellan is not using the Army, I should like to borrow it for a while."

Later in a letter to McClellan trying to urge the general into action, he wrote, "I say 'try;' if we never try, we shall never succeed."

Too often we become paralyzed by fear.

In McClellan's case, he kept telling Lincoln he wasn't ready yet. He had to train his army, first. And, after he trained his army, he became unsure he had the proper supplies to go into battle, and chase after his enemies. Then he needed more men, because he thought the enemy had him out soldiered.

Lincoln's answer to him was simple and to the point, "Why did he think he couldn't do what his opponent was managing to do so well every day."

How often do your salesmen tell you they're out maneuvered, or out priced, by the competition? Our competitor has a lower price, they have a broader selection, they have better financing, free deliver, whatever the supposed barrier may be.

Remember Lincoln's words, "if we never try, we shall never succeed…"

Sometimes the hardest part of the battle is getting started. You're always going to be outgunned on something, get your people out there trying. The successes will follow.

Don't worry about what you didn't say

Secretary of the Treasury, Salmon P. Chase, remarked to Lincoln, "Oh, I am so sorry that I did not write a letter to Mr. So-and-so before I left home."

President Lincoln promptly responded:

"Chase, never regret what you don't write; it is what you do write that you are often called upon to feel sorry."

Too many times people feel sorry, for not saying something they wished they had said, but the real problem is when you open your mouth and say the wrong thing. Then, you have a heap of "explaining to do."

Worry about what you say.

Every mouth should come with the warning: Careful what comes out of here. It's oftentimes difficult to put your words back in.

How many times have you started talking, and thought, "Oh my God! Why did I say that?" The real problem is our tongues often get to wagging, before our brain gets to thinking.

Back in the days when I used to do an honest day's work, my boss always warned me I was "my own worst enemy." I just couldn't keep my mouth shut.

Lincoln was definitely right; you will very seldom find yourself regretting what you didn't say.

Call a spade, a spade

President Lincoln had great doubt as to his right to emancipate the slaves under war power. In discussing the question, he used to liken the case to that of the boy who when asked how many legs his calf would have if he called the tail a leg, replied 'five:' to which the prompt response was made that calling the tail a leg would not make it a leg.

In telling this story Lincoln emphasized a thing "is what it is." Just because you call it something different, doesn't make it so.

How many times have you found yourself on the losing end of an argument trying to defend something that had no defense?

Ronald Reagan tried to say "ketchup" was a vegetable when discussing the school lunch program, but try as he could to defend it, it was still just a condiment you put on a burger.

If you really want to defend something, defend it for what it is, not for what you want it to be.

Enough said.

What's more important?

One day Lincoln received news about the capture of 100 horses and several brigadier-generals on a Virginia battlefield. The President is said to have responded, "Sorry about the horses, I can make more brigadier-generals."

The president later apologized for his inconsiderate sounding remark, but told his companion the horses cost him $100 each.

You've got to know what's important. Lincoln had people approaching him every day about the possibility of being appointed a brigadier-general. Horses were a whole other story. They cost him money, and that was something he never had enough of to run the war properly.

When you're running a business, you need to be able to prioritize. Sure, losing the generals was a blow to Lincoln, but in the big scheme of things, he had a long string of applicants who wanted to become brigadier-generals, very few horses were volunteering to be shot at the front.

What's your hot button?

Change your thought, change your mindset

In one of his letters, Lincoln wrote:

"When one is embarrassed, usually the shortest way to get through with it, is to quit talking or thinking about it, and go to something else."

Got something on your mind that just won't stop bothering you? Sometimes the best way to stop worrying about it is to start thinking about something else.

Let me tell you what I mean. Recently a local grocery store was the subject of a cyber-heist where the bandits stole their customer's credit card numbers. The company's response was to put their president all over the media – TV, radio, and newspaper advertisements, saying how sorry he was for the incident, and how they had taken steps to make sure it wouldn't happen again.

Now I know transparency with your customers is the latest trend and all, but the company's approach opened them up to an entirely new audience that didn't know anything about what happened.

A better approach would have been to be totally honest with the affected customers, while not sharing what happened with the rest of the world.

Sure the company was embarrassed by what happened, or perhaps more so, by how it made them look in the media. The problem is their response, only made the problem known to more people.

You can fool some of the people

"It is true that you may fool all of the people some of the time; you can even fool some of the people all of the time; but you can't fool all of the people all the time."

This is probably one of Lincoln's most popular sayings.

Sure you can fool people some of the time, but eventually they're going to catch you.

Be honest in what you do. Don't make exaggerated claims about what you're going to do, or what your product can do. Truth really is the best answer.

Do unto others

Doctor Jerome Walker tells of the time he was rebuked by President Lincoln. He was showing the President through City Point Hospital, and after they had visited all of the wards, they came to the final area.

The doctor told Lincoln he probably wouldn't want to visit these wards, "they are only rebels."

Lincoln gently rested his large hand on the doctor's shoulder, and said, "You mean Confederates."

After hearing those words, the doctor had no choice but to take Lincoln through those three wards. He was surprised to see that Lincoln was as friendly with the Confederate wounded, as with his own. He made his way through the ward, shaking hands and sharing stories with everyone there.

Treat your enemies (competitors) like you would your friends.

While everyone else was focused on winning the war, Lincoln was focused on the big goal: Bringing the country back together. He knew there was no difference between the wounded prisoners, and those from his own army. As such he treated them equally.

How about you? Do you treat your competition like the enemy? Or are you friendly with them?

Chances are you're going to see a lot of your competition. You're going to meet up with them at trade shows, when you're visiting customers, and at recruiting fairs.

If you haven't done so yet, strike up a conversation with them, and share a little information that can help both of you run your business better.

No man is irreplaceable

Salmon P. Chase, when Secretary of the Treasury, had a disagreement with other members of the Cabinet and resigned.

The President was urged not to accept it, as "Secretary Chase is today a national necessity," his advisers said.

"How mistaken you are!" Lincoln quietly observed. "Yet it is not strange; I used to have similar notions. No! If we should all be turned out tomorrow, and could come back here in a week, we should find our places filled by a lot of fellows doing just as well as we did, and in many instances better.

"Now, this reminds me of what the Irishman said. His verdict was that "in this country one man is as good as another; and, for the matter of that, very often a great deal better. No, this Government does not depend upon the life of any many.

A lot of people come to think, for one reason or another they are irreplaceable.

Lincoln knew better. There is always somebody else out there just as able, and ready to take over.

Many people fool themselves, and think they are irreplaceable because they've been on the job for so long, or because they know the job better than anyone else, or because they know everyone in the company. The truth, however, is something totally different.

All of us are replaceable.

Especially in today's economy, there are thousands of people out there with the same skills and backgrounds you have. Many of them may even be more qualified than you are.

The next time you get to thinking that you're irreplaceable, start thinking about what else you can do to ensure your company won't want to replace you. That's the real secret to becoming irreplaceable. Keep upgrading your skills.

Lincoln's management style

When Lincoln assumed the Presidency he had many doubts about his abilities. He'd never been a Governor or Cabinet member, he didn't know anything about international politics or the military, and yet here he was in the highest office in the land.

The country he took over was being split apart by the slavery issue, and even before he had been inaugurated as President, eight states had seceded from the Union. His predecessor, James Buchanan, had taken no action on any of these issues, instead leaving the incoming Lincoln to deal with them all.

His welcome to the Presidency was made worse by being forced to sneak into the Capital City under the cover of darkness, because of a suspected plot to assassinate him. At the time of his arrival, Washington was rife with rumors of assassinations, and kidnappings, and conspiracies to blowup or lay siege to the city.

No President, before or since, has assumed power under such tenuous circumstances.

Mr. Lincoln was forced to grow up fast. In a matter of months he was transformed from a frontier politician, into a national leader.

As with every position, he hit some rough spots, some of them almost cost him the Presidency, and others, the country. Often times during his first few years as

President, Lincoln was the most reviled man in the country, hated and cursed by his friends and his enemies.

Despite all of this, he taught himself about politics, and about the military, until he could be the leader he needed to be.

Here's how Lincoln managed his soldiers, and his generals.

Lincoln and the soldiers

No President, other than possibly, George Washington, was more intimate with his soldiers.

By early 1862, Washington was filled with Army hospitals. Wounded soldiers were housed in churches, and schools, and cities of white hospital tents dotted the landscape everywhere. Wounded soldiers walked through the city and were drawn into the hospitals on carts.

Congressmen spent most of every Saturday and Sunday in the hospitals, visiting with soldiers from their districts. They comforted the soldiers, wrote letters home for them, and swapped stories with them.

Prominent among the hospital visitors was Abraham Lincoln. He was a constant visitor to his wounded soldiers, sharing stories, and doing what he could to cheer them up. Many stories are told of Lincoln holding a bedside vigil, and weeping over the dying soldiers.

On the streets, Lincoln always took time out to greet the soldiers he passed by, shaking their hands, and asking about them and their families.

On his many battlefield visits, Lincoln made it a point to meet with the soldiers, and encourage them however he could. Hundreds of soldiers shared their stories with Lincoln's biographers, describing "Old Abe's" visits, and how he took the time to talk with them, and about the stories he told.

His wife, Mary Todd Lincoln, worked in the hospitals comforting the soldiers, and doing what she could to ensure they had proper food, and supplies.

But, perhaps, the closest relations Lincoln had with the soldiers were with the guards at his summer cottage at the Soldier's Home outside of Washington. The guards were represented by Company K of the 150th Pennsylvania Volunteers under Captain D. V. Derickson. Lincoln often rode there alone at night, to unwind after a hard day's work.

Lincoln's son, Tad, spent much of his time there, and had an honorary lieutenant's commission in the regiment. Mary Lincoln took it upon herself to see the guard's at the Soldier's Home had turkey dinner every Thanksgiving. Derickson's men boasted Lincoln knew each of them by name.

Every day Lincoln was approached by the mothers, fathers, brothers, or sisters, of soldiers about to be executed for desertion or for falling asleep at their post. Lincoln would listen quietly, as the relatives plead their case, and in just about every instance he was moved towards leniency.

Lincoln's normal message was "Suspend execution of death sentence until further orders."

One father seeing those words complained to Lincoln, "but that doesn't pardon my boy." To which the President replied, "My dear man, do you suppose I will ever give orders for your boy's execution?"

There are thousands of instances where Lincoln refused to allow soldiers to be executed. His thinking was for many, they were just boys, away from home for the first time, and they couldn't help falling asleep at their post, or being homesick. It was just too much for Lincoln to order the death sentence for them.

Lincoln's thought on the matter was, "I never felt sure but I might drop my gun and run away if I found myself in the line of battle." The man might be poor and friendless. "If he has no friends, I'll be his friend," said Lincoln. "Suspend execution, send me his record," was the President's order.

If you can learn only one thing from Lincoln's management style with his soldiers, make it this: Have compassion for your employees, and don't judge them without first standing in their shoes for a minute.

Lincoln understood that to inspire confidence among the troops he had to spend time among them, and this he did in the streets of Washington, in the army hospitals, and on the battlefields.

If you want to inspire confidence in your employees, the way Lincoln did with his soldiers spend the majority of your time working with them, sharing stories, shaking hands, and understanding what you are asking them to do.

Lincoln and his generals

Lincoln had many problems with his generals, especially at the beginning of the war. The most frustrating of which was their inaction.

From the start of the war, General McClellan proved to be a thorn in Lincoln's side. Lincoln waited patiently for McClellan to build and train his army, and when that was done, he expected him to go into battle. But, McClellan hesitated so much, Lincoln began calling the Army of the Potomac, "McClellan's bodyguard." For his part, the general showed outright contempt for Lincoln, several times refusing to receive him when he visited his camp.

On September 17th, McClellan overtook Lee's army at Antietam, and defeated him. But, instead of following up on his victory, and going after Lee's retreating army, McClellan stayed in camp.

Lincoln was so frustrated by this failure to act he visited McClellan on the battlefield in October. He was determined to find out for himself, the state of his army, and see for himself if McClellan was right that he lacked the proper materials to pursue Lee.

What he found was: McClellan surrounded by 100,000 men, once again acting as his personal bodyguard. Lincoln personally surveyed the camp. He interviewed generals, visited the hospitals, and talked with the soldiers. The day after he returned to Washington, he sent McClellan the following order, "The President directs that you cross the Potomac and give battle to the enemy or drive him south."

A week later, McClellan had not budged from his position. Lincoln wrote him again, "You remember my speaking to you of what I called your over-cautiousness? Are you not over-cautious when you assume that you cannot do what the enemy is constantly doing?"

The tactful letter did not move McClellan to action. Instead, he wrote Lincoln his "cavalry horses had sore tongues."

Lincoln telegraphed back that, "I have just read your dispatch about sore-tongued and fatigued horses. Will you pardon me for asking what the horses of your army have done since the Battle of Antietam that fatigues anything?"

Finally on the first of November, Lincoln gave up hope for McClellan and removed him from command of the army.

After this he appointed General Burnside, who shortly thereafter went into battle with Lee at

Fredericksburg. The results were disastrous for the Union troops with over 10,000 dead.

Afraid to let Burnside go into another battle, Lincoln put Fighting Joe Hooker in charge but felt it his duty to first write Hooker about some of his misgivings in appointing him. Hooker's response to the letter was recorded by Noah Brooks –

"He finished reading it, almost with tears in his eyes; and as he folded it and put it back into the breast of his coat, he said, 'That is just such a letter as a father might write to a son. It is a beautiful letter, and although I think he was harder on me than I deserve, I will say that I love the man who wrote it.'"

Shortly thereafter Hooker went into battle and was pushed back beyond the Rappahannock. He resigned (after being criticized for his performance), and was replaced by General Meade.

Meade immediately engaged with Lee at the Gettysburg, winning a great victory for the Union troops. Despite the victory, Lincoln could only feel discouraged, because Meade failed to chase Lee down, and claim a decisive victory.

Lincoln telegraphed Meade the following message –

"I do not believe you appreciate the magnitude of the misfortune involved in Lee's escape. He was within your easy grasp, and to have closed upon him would, in connection with our other late successes, have ended the war. As it is, the war will be prolonged indefinitely…

"I beg you not to consider this a prosecution or persecution of yourself. As you had learned that I was dissatisfied, I have thought it best to kindly tell you why."

Finally, Lincoln set his eyes upon General Ulysses S. Grant, as a candidate for Commander-in-Chief of his army, but before making a move, he sent newspaperman, Charles A. Dana to observe Grant on the battlefield, and learn what he could about the man.

Dana confirmed his choice. Grant was steadily working his way along the Mississippi, taking Donelson then Vicksburg, and with that done he immediately made plans for his next battle.

Lincoln search was over. He had found his new hard charging commander of the army. Grant was a focused bull-dog whose determination won the war for Lincoln.

***

I apologize for the history lesson, but Lincoln's search for a new general to command his army tells us a lot about the man, and his management style.

1) Lincoln was a hand's on leader. When he couldn't get the information he wanted, he visited the battlefields and surveyed the scene for himself.

2) Lincoln didn't just talk to his generals he visited the wounded in the hospitals, and the soldiers in the field to solicit their opinions.

3) Lincoln didn't make rash decisions. He took the time to try and understand the situations facing his generals, and to determine if there was anything he could do to help them.

4) Lincoln at all times kept his cool, and treated his generals with respect and dignity, even when he was totally frustrated with their action, or lack thereof.

5) Lincoln studied the details of what was going on at the battlefields, but he understood the big picture as well. What frustrated him most was there were several instances where his generals were on the verge of totally defeating the Confederacy, and stopped short, thus prolonging the war.

The final takeaway is: Don't be afraid to visit the front. Get out there and work with your managers, and learn for yourself what's going on in their work environment.

A lot of companies today run through management teams, like they're change clothes. At the first sign of bad news, or unsatisfactory numbers, they rush to assemble the newest dream team. Lincoln gave all of his generals every chance he could. Often times he took the blame for their failures, while encouraging them to succeed. Before determining that you need to replace someone, see what you can do to help them succeed.

If you do all of these things, and you will be able to manage like Abraham Lincoln.

www.ingramcontent.com/pod-product-compliance
Lightning Source LLC
Chambersburg PA
CBHW051224170526
45166CB00005B/2027